MAYER SMITH

A Dance with the Firestorm Prince

Copyright © 2025 by Mayer Smith

All rights reserved. No part of this publication may be reproduced, stored or transmitted in any form or by any means, electronic, mechanical, photocopying, recording, scanning, or otherwise without written permission from the publisher. It is illegal to copy this book, post it to a website, or distribute it by any other means without permission.

This novel is entirely a work of fiction. The names, characters and incidents portrayed in it are the work of the author's imagination. Any resemblance to actual persons, living or dead, events or localities is entirely coincidental.

Mayer Smith asserts the moral right to be identified as the author of this work.

Mayer Smith has no responsibility for the persistence or accuracy of URLs for external or third-party Internet Websites referred to in this publication and does not guarantee that any content on such Websites is, or will remain, accurate or appropriate.

Designations used by companies to distinguish their products are often claimed as trademarks. All brand names and product names used in this book and on its cover are trade names, service marks, trademarks and registered trademarks of their respective owners. The publishers and the book are not associated with any product or vendor mentioned in this book. None of the companies referenced within the book have endorsed the book.

First edition

This book was professionally typeset on Reedsy. Find out more at reedsy.com

Contents

1	Embers in the Wind	1
2	Ashes and Allegiances	7
3	A Bargain in the Dark	14
4	Burn	21
5	The Dance of Lies	27
6	The Flames of Betrayal	33
7	Chains of Duty	39
8	The Inferno Within	45
9	The Forbidden Bond	51
10	The Inferno Within	57
11	Chapter 11	64
12	Dance	70

One

Embers in the Wind

The music swelled, a haunting melody spun from the fingers of the royal musicians, threading through the grand ballroom like a whispered spell. The chandeliers above dripped with golden firelight, casting flickering shadows that seemed to dance upon the polished marble floors.

Liora took her place at the center of the opulent room, her silk dress clinging to her form like liquid dusk. The fabric shimmered as she moved, a thousand silver threads woven through deep indigo, reflecting the glow of the torches lining the walls. She had danced for nobles before, for men in embroidered coats who cared little for the art and more for the allure of a woman's body in motion. But tonight was different.

Tonight, he was watching.

A Dance with the Firestorm Prince

She had felt his gaze long before she found him in the crowd. It burned like a brand at the nape of her neck, a searing awareness that unsettled her more than the jeweled masks and unreadable faces surrounding her. Liora did not let it show.

She lifted her arms, her body bending into the first movement of the dance, a tale of longing and loss. Her bare feet brushed against the cool marble, each step measured, deliberate. The air seemed charged with something electric, something that made her heart beat too fast, though the room was silent but for the rise and fall of the melody.

And then—she saw him.

A figure leaned against one of the grand pillars that framed the ballroom, half-draped in shadow, watching her with an intensity that sent a slow, crawling shiver down her spine. Unlike the other guests, whose silk and finery shone in ostentatious wealth, he wore black, the high collar of his coat lined with flame-colored embroidery, subtle yet unmistakable. His face was obscured by a mask of onyx and gold, cut in sharp, angular lines that only emphasized the predator beneath it.

But it was his eyes that caught her—piercing, molten, like embers smoldering beneath an unbroken surface.

The Firestorm Prince.

Liora forced herself to continue dancing, though the air in her lungs felt tight, like a storm was pressing against her ribs. Why was he here?

Embers in the Wind

The kingdom of Vareth was no friend to the Firestorm Throne. Whispers of war had spread like wildfire across the courts, and yet here he stood, unbothered, observing her as if he had already conquered the space around him.

And still—his gaze never wavered.

Liora spun, her skirts flaring, the rapid drumbeat of her heart matching the rhythm of the music. She had been trained to captivate, to lure, to make her audience forget everything but the way she moved. And yet, she had never before felt like prey.

The song reached its crescendo, and as she came to her final pose, a thunderous applause erupted. The nobles clapped politely, some whispering, some leering, but Liora barely heard them. Her breath came in quiet gasps as she finally lifted her chin and met his gaze head-on.

For a moment, neither of them moved.

And then, with the ghost of a smirk, he turned and disappeared into the crowd.

A Warning Dressed in Silk

The evening pressed on with glittering conversations and false laughter. Liora stood near the silk-draped alcoves, forcing herself to sip from the goblet of spiced wine a noble had pressed into her hands.

Her nerves were still frayed.

A Dance with the Firestorm Prince

She had heard of Prince Kael, the Firestorm heir. He was not just a prince—he was a living weapon, the blood of the Phoenix Kings running through his veins. Some said his rage could turn men to cinders with a glance, that the air shimmered with heat when he was near.

She had never thought she would stand in the same room as him.

"You dance like someone who knows the weight of chains."

Liora tensed at the deep voice behind her, its tone rich, smooth—dangerous.

She turned.

Kael stood before her, closer now, the mask still in place but unable to hide the sharpness of his gaze. He studied her, not like a noble admiring a performer, but like a scholar unraveling a mystery.

Liora did not let herself shrink beneath it. "You speak like a man who knows what it's like to wear them."

His lips curled, the barest hint of amusement. "Perhaps."

The room felt too small. The scent of burning cedar clung to him, like the memory of an extinguished fire, lingering but never truly gone.

"You shouldn't be here," she said softly, fingers tightening around her goblet.

"Neither should you," he murmured. "And yet, here we are."

A shiver traced her spine, though the air was warm.

He leaned in, not touching her, but close enough that she could feel the heat radiating from his body. "They don't deserve you, these men in their gilded masks." His voice was low, meant only for her. "They see a dancer. But I see something else."

Liora swallowed, pulse hammering. "And what is that?"

"Someone who does not belong in a cage."

His words unsettled her, not because they were untrue, but because they felt too close to something she had tried so hard to bury.

"Stay away from me, Prince Kael," she whispered. "Our kingdoms are at the edge of war. If they see us speaking, it will be dangerous for both of us."

Kael tilted his head, as if considering her words. "And yet, I find danger... intoxicating."

Liora exhaled sharply, shaking her head, willing herself to move past him. But as she did, he reached out—just barely—fingers brushing the bare skin of her wrist. The contact was brief, but it burned, a sensation that did not fade even when she put distance between them.

A Dance with the Firestorm Prince

When she finally dared to glance back, Kael was gone.

But the air still carried the embers of his presence.

And deep in her heart, Liora knew this was not the last time their paths would cross.

A storm was coming.

And she had just danced into the fire.

Two

Ashes and Allegiances

The cold sting of moonlight draped over the empty corridors of the palace. The sound of distant laughter and clinking goblets still echoed through the grand hall, but here, away from the gilded chandeliers and intoxicating perfumes, the air was thin.

Liora moved with silent urgency, her skirts gathered in one hand, the other tracing the edges of the stone walls to steady herself. She had danced, smiled, and played the role expected of her, but something in the Firestorm Prince's words lingered, curling inside her mind like smoke refusing to clear.

"Someone who does not belong in a cage."

It was dangerous to let his voice settle in her thoughts.

She needed to leave. The ball had long since ended, and she had overstayed her welcome in a palace where whispers could turn into daggers. The nobles of Vareth would already be murmuring about her exchange with Kael. She could not afford suspicion.

Liora rounded the corner, her breath steady but her heartbeat erratic. She would take the servants' passage to the back gardens, slip through the hedge maze, and be gone before anyone noticed her absence.

But as she reached the archway leading to the outer halls, a voice—sharp and laced with authority—halted her in her tracks.

"Dancer."

Her spine stiffened. Slowly, she turned.

Lord Carraven stood before her, flanked by two guards. He was a man of lean build, his features chiseled like marble, devoid of warmth. His deep red robe, embroidered with the sigil of the ruling house, billowed slightly as he stepped forward. His gaze, cool and calculating, settled on her with quiet menace.

"You should not be wandering the palace alone," he said, his tone calm but edged with something far more dangerous.

Liora forced herself to bow, a dancer's bow—low, graceful, obedient. "Forgive me, my lord. I was only taking my leave."

Carraven's gaze did not waver. He lifted a gloved hand, rubbing his fingers together as if considering something distasteful. "You have drawn attention to yourself tonight."

Liora remained still, though every muscle in her body urged her to flee.

Carraven's lips curled into something that did not quite reach a smile. "You danced well. Too well, I think."

A slow chill traced her spine.

"You caught the eye of the Firestorm Prince." He said it like an accusation, not a statement. His eyes flickered with something unreadable, something cold and dissecting. "That is a problem."

Liora inhaled sharply. "I—"

"Silence." His voice cut through the air, and for the first time, true fear gripped her.

Carraven stepped closer, his presence coiling around her like a serpent. "You are not one of us. You are not of noble blood, nor do you hold a place in this court beyond fleeting entertainment. And yet, tonight, you placed yourself in the path of a man who could burn this kingdom to the ground."

Liora clenched her jaw. She had no words that would satisfy him, no explanation that would make her seem less of a threat.

Carraven tilted his head, as if he could read her silence like an open book. "We do not take kindly to women who think themselves above their station."

She braced herself, expecting the command—Arrest her. Detain her. Dispose of her.

Instead, Carraven lifted his hand in a slow, deliberate gesture. The guards moved toward her.

Liora turned to run.

A hand clamped around her wrist—too strong, too sudden.

She gasped, struggling, but the grip was unyielding. Panic coiled in her chest as the guards seized her arms.

"My lord—"

Her protest was cut short as one of the guards pulled something from his belt—a thin, silken cloth soaked in something pungent.

She barely had time to react before it was pressed against her lips and nose.

The scent hit her like a wave, sharp and dizzying.

Her limbs weakened. Her breath faltered.

Darkness rushed in.

Shadows and Flames
  Heat.

Ashes and Allegiances

That was the first thing she noticed.

It was not the heat of the ballroom or the warmth of candlelight—it was something alive, something smoldering just beneath her skin.

Her consciousness flickered like a dying flame, wavering between wakefulness and the black void that tried to pull her under. There was motion, the sensation of being carried, the distant sound of a horse's hooves against the ground.

Her mind screamed at her to wake.

Liora forced her eyes open.

The world tilted. She was draped across the saddle of a horse, her body bound, her wrists tied with rough rope. The night sky stretched above her, silver-lined clouds barely concealing the crescent moon. A cold wind lashed against her exposed skin, but the warmth—the heat—came from beside her.

From him.

Prince Kael rode beside her, his dark cloak rippling behind him, his hands steady on the reins of his steed. His onyx and gold mask was gone, revealing a face carved from shadows and firelight. His jaw was sharp, his expression unreadable. The only thing alive about him were his eyes—molten, seething, intense.

Liora's pulse pounded in her ears. "What have you done?" Her voice was hoarse, slurred from the remnants of the drug.

Kael didn't look at her immediately. When he did, there was no amusement in his gaze, none of the teasing arrogance from earlier.

"I just saved your life."

Liora struggled against the ropes. "You kidnapped me."

"If I hadn't, you'd be dead."

She stopped struggling.

Kael exhaled, rubbing his temple as if speaking to her required patience he did not have. "Carraven wouldn't have let you leave that palace alive. You caught my attention, and that alone was enough to sign your death warrant."

Liora's breath hitched. The truth of his words settled into her bones.

"Where are you taking me?" she demanded.

Kael's lips pressed into a firm line. "Somewhere safer than where you were."

She did not trust him. She could not. And yet—he had pulled her from something far worse.

Liora stared at him, at the way the firelight from his horse's lantern reflected in his gaze.

"You expect me to believe you're my savior?" she whispered.

Kael turned to her fully then, his expression unreadable. And for the first time, she noticed something beneath his hardened exterior—something flickering just beneath the surface.

"No," he said softly. "I expect you to survive."

The wind howled between them as the horses carried them deeper into the unknown.

Liora had stepped into the fire.

And now, there was no turning back.

Three

A Bargain in the Dark

The night stretched endlessly, an ink-black abyss pressing against the world as Liora fought the haze still lingering in her mind. The rhythmic pounding of the horses' hooves against the dirt road echoed through the silence, a steady drumbeat that matched the erratic pulse hammering in her chest.

The ropes around her wrists burned, chafing against her skin each time she moved. Her body ached from being slung over the saddle, but the heat—his heat—was the most unnerving of all. Kael rode beside her, his presence like a living flame, a steady source of warmth in the biting night air.

She had been stolen from the palace. Stolen from everything she knew.

A Bargain in the Dark

And yet, a whisper of something dark and treacherous stirred inside her.

She had also been saved.

The thought made her grit her teeth.

Liora shifted, trying to ease the discomfort in her muscles. "Untie me."

Kael's gaze flickered toward her, unreadable in the dim glow of the lantern swaying from his saddle. "Not yet."

Her fingers curled into fists. "You expect me to trust you after you bound me like a prisoner?"

"No." His voice was calm, maddeningly so. "But I expect you to listen."

Liora let out a sharp, humorless laugh. "You are either arrogant or foolish if you think I will sit here and have a conversation like we are old friends."

Kael reined in his horse, forcing it to slow. Liora's own horse came to a halt beside his, and the world fell into silence, save for the rustling of the wind through the trees. The scent of damp earth and pine filled the air, mixing with the ever-present scent of burning cedar that clung to him.

He turned toward her, his gaze intense in the lantern's glow. "You want to go back?"

Liora swallowed hard. The memory of Carraven's cold voice, the guards' hands pinning her down, the press of the cloth over her mouth—it all came rushing back, and for a moment, she felt the phantom grip of fear closing around her throat.

Kael watched her carefully, as if reading every flicker of emotion across her face. "I didn't take you to hurt you, Liora. I took you because you were already a marked woman the moment I looked at you."

Something in his tone sent a shiver through her, an unsettling mix of warning and promise.

Liora forced herself to meet his gaze. "Then why not let me go now?"

Kael exhaled, shifting slightly in his saddle. "Because you are more than just a dancer."

The words sent an unsteady ripple through her.

She laughed, the sound brittle. "Oh? And what am I, then? A pawn in your political games?"

Kael's gaze darkened, but not with anger—with something worse.

"An answer," he said simply.

The response sent a chill down her spine.

Liora shook her head. "You're speaking in riddles, and I don't have the patience for it."

Kael studied her for a long moment before swinging down from his horse. He landed gracefully, the movement fluid, as if the earth bent to his will. Then, without another word, he reached up and untied the ropes securing her wrists.

Liora didn't hesitate. The moment her hands were free, she moved to dismount. But as soon as her feet hit the ground, her knees nearly buckled.

Kael's hand shot out, gripping her elbow before she could stumble.

His touch burned.

Liora jerked away, breath unsteady. "Don't touch me."

Kael didn't argue, simply stepping back. His expression was unreadable, but something flickered in his gaze, something that made her stomach tighten in a way she did not want to acknowledge.

"We should keep moving," he said after a beat. "We're not safe here."

She narrowed her eyes. "We? I didn't ask to be part of we."

Kael let out a low chuckle, and something about the sound sent a ripple of frustration through her. "And yet, here we are."

Liora turned, casting a quick glance at the darkened woods around them. The road stretched endlessly in both directions, disappearing into the shadows. She had no idea where they were or how far they had traveled.

If she ran, would she make it?

Kael sighed, as if sensing the question forming in her mind. "You could try to run. But you won't make it far before someone finds you. And believe me, not everyone is as kind as I am."

Liora scoffed. "You call this kindness?"

Kael smirked, tilting his head. "Would you prefer I had left you to Carraven?"

Silence.

Liora hated that she had no answer.

Kael stepped closer, not enough to touch, but enough to let her feel the heat radiating from him. "I have a proposition for you."

She clenched her jaw. "I want no part of your kingdom's affairs."

Kael ignored the protest. "You have a gift."

Liora stiffened. "A gift?"

He nodded. "You don't see it yet, but I do. The way you moved tonight—it wasn't just a dance. The very air around you responded to it."

Liora frowned. "That's absurd."

Kael's lips curled, but it wasn't amusement. It was something darker.

"Is it?" He stepped even closer, voice low, coaxing. "Tell me, Liora—have you never felt it? The way the earth shifts beneath your feet when you move? The way the wind bends to you?"

A chill rippled through her.

Because she had.

Small things. The way the ground seemed more alive beneath her feet when she danced in open fields. The way the air pulsed around her when she lost herself in movement. The way the world listened when she let go.

She had always dismissed it as coincidence.

Liora inhaled sharply. "Even if I believed you—which I don't—why would that matter to you?"

Kael's gaze burned. "Because my kingdom is at war. And you may be the key to ending it."

The weight of his words pressed against her like a storm waiting to break.

Liora wanted to deny him. Wanted to call him a liar, a manipulator, a man who played with fire and expected not to be burned.

But the truth hung heavy in the air.

Something was happening.

Something far bigger than she understood.

And somehow, she was tangled in it.

Kael watched her carefully, his expression unreadable. "Help me, and I will help you."

Liora swallowed, her heart pounding.

A prince's bargain.

A firestorm waiting to consume her.

And yet, as she stared into his ember-lit gaze, she knew—this was only the beginning.

Four

Burn

The journey had felt like an eternity, a slow, unyielding march into the unknown. Liora's muscles ached from the long ride, her body stiff from hours of motion, the remnants of the cold rope still biting into her skin. Yet, it wasn't the physical exhaustion that unsettled her—it was the burning tension that swirled between her and the prince, that constant undercurrent of something she couldn't name.

Kael remained a silent presence beside her, his figure cutting through the night like an untamed storm. His eyes—those smoldering embers—never strayed from the road ahead, but Liora could feel him watching her in the same way a hawk watches its prey. He said nothing, but the weight of his attention was a constant force, pressing down on her, making the air between them thick and suffocating.

They rode through dense forests, the trees towering like ancient guardians in the night, their branches swaying softly in the breeze. The scent of pine mixed with the faintest trace of smoke, and the sound of the horses' hooves softened as they crossed over thick, moss-covered ground. Still, Liora couldn't escape the feeling that she was being led deeper into something dark, something that would not easily release its grip on her.

The fire inside her chest, the heat she couldn't quite explain, flared to life again. Kael's presence seemed to stoke the flames, each movement he made—a brush of his fingers against his reins, a shift of his cloak in the wind—sending a tremor through her. She tried to ignore it, tried to focus on the path ahead, but her thoughts kept circling back to him.

Finally, after what seemed like an eternity, they reached a clearing—a small, secluded valley where the moonlight filtered down through the canopy of trees. The horses slowed, their breath visible in the cool night air as they came to a stop. Kael dismounted first, fluidly and with the grace of a predator, before turning to offer his hand to Liora.

Her heart beat faster at the gesture, but she hesitated.

"Come," Kael said, his voice low, almost soothing. "It's safer here."

Safer? Liora almost laughed, but there was something in his tone—something urgent, something that made her hesitate. The world around her was silent except for the whisper of the wind, and beneath that silence, she felt something else.

Something watching.

She took his hand.

The moment their skin touched, something crackled between them—an electric pulse that made her breath catch in her throat. She felt it from the tips of her fingers all the way to her spine, a shock of heat that sent a tremor through her body. She quickly pulled her hand away, but the warmth lingered, like a brand, a reminder that she was caught in something far greater than herself.

Kael's expression softened, just a little, but the intensity in his eyes never wavered. He turned and led her toward a small campfire, its flames dancing and flickering in the dark, casting long shadows on the ground. The warmth of the fire was a welcome relief after the cold bite of the night air, but it did nothing to quell the unease crawling up her spine.

Liora sat down on a bed of soft moss, her body tense as she watched him move around the camp, setting up the horses and arranging a simple meal. She should've felt safe, but every part of her screamed that something was wrong. There was too much darkness in the world she had stepped into.

She couldn't help herself—her eyes kept drifting to him. Kael moved like a force of nature, his every step calculated, purposeful. His cloak billowed behind him like the wings of a bird of prey, and his posture—so commanding, so sure—made him seem more like a king than the prince he was.

"You know," Liora said, her voice quieter than she intended, "I've never been one to believe in prophecies."

Kael paused, turning his head slightly to look at her, his dark eyes piercing in the firelight. "No?"

"I thought they were stories. Folklore. Things meant to keep children awake at night." She shrugged, though her fingers gripped the edges of her dress tightly, betraying her nervousness. "But I'm beginning to think there's truth in them after all."

His gaze deepened, unreadable. "Prophecies are rarely what they seem." He bent down, retrieving a small bundle of dried herbs from his pack, his back to her. "But you've felt it, haven't you? The way the earth shifts when you move. The way the air around you reacts."

Liora frowned, her breath catching. "I don't know what you're talking about."

Kael turned to face her then, the firelight casting strange shadows on his face, making him look both human and other—a being not entirely bound by the earth beneath their feet. His eyes were molten, flames dancing in them, and for a moment, Liora wondered if he could truly see the power inside her, the power she had always kept hidden.

"I know you feel it," Kael said softly. "The way you can make the world bend to you. To your will."

Liora shook her head, but it was harder this time. Her mind raced, her pulse quickening. It was true—she had felt it, but she had always thought it was nothing more than instinct. An odd, fleeting sensation. Something that could be ignored. But Kael's words, his certainty, made it impossible to deny any longer.

"You're wrong," she said, though her voice wavered.

Kael's lips curled into a faint, knowing smile. "Am I?"

The air between them seemed to grow thicker, charged with an electric current that she couldn't escape. It wasn't just the power he spoke of—there was something else between them. A connection, maybe, or something darker, something that made her feel both terrified and alive.

Kael straightened, his eyes never leaving hers. "I don't need you to believe me. But I do need you to help me."

Liora stiffened. "Help you with what?"

Kael knelt beside her, close enough that she could feel the heat radiating off him, the warmth from the fire mixing with the warmth of his presence. His voice dropped to a whisper. "I need you to help me awaken what lies dormant inside you. What could end this war."

Liora swallowed, her throat dry. "I don't know what you're talking about."

He leaned in slightly, his face inches from hers, and the sudden proximity sent a jolt of heat through her veins. "You will. You'll understand soon enough. And when you do, there will be no turning back."

A strange, almost magnetic force pulled at her, urging her to trust him. But she knew better than to follow that instinct. She had no place in this world, no place in his plans. She was nothing more than a tool, a means to an end. And yet, his words, his touch, sent her thoughts spiraling.

"Why me?" she whispered. "Why not someone else?"

Kael's gaze softened, and for a fleeting moment, she saw something else in his eyes—something human. A flicker of vulnerability that she wasn't sure she could trust.

"Because, Liora," he said softly, his voice a mere breath against her ear, "you and I are the same."

The words hung in the air, heavy with meaning. They were a promise. And a curse.

The fire crackled between them, its flames licking at the night air, but it wasn't the fire that was burning. It was something deeper, something that would consume them both.

And as Liora stared into Kael's molten eyes, she knew—she had already stepped into the flames.

Five

The Dance of Lies

The sound of footsteps echoed softly through the grand stone hallway, each step deliberate and measured. Liora's heart pounded in her chest, the rhythm of it quick and erratic like the flutter of wings against her ribs. She paused before the heavy wooden door, her breath shallow as she tried to steady herself. The moment had arrived. The moment where she would step from the shadows and into a world that she had never belonged to.

She adjusted the dark blue silk of her dress, the color a subtle but deliberate contrast to the vivid red and gold of the court's nobility. The fabric clung to her like water, wrapping around her form in a way that made every movement feel deliberate, every gesture, a whisper of something that was about to be revealed. She had danced for them before—the nobles, the faceless men who saw her as nothing more than a thing to be admired, consumed, and discarded—but this was different. Tonight, the stakes were far higher.

Liora closed her eyes for a brief moment, allowing herself to breathe in the scent of the evening—wax from the candles, the faint trace of incense, and the rich aroma of food that filled the air. But beneath it all, there was something darker, something she could not name that clung to the air like smoke. She had never felt more out of place, and yet she could not deny the pull, the magnetism that had begun to form between herself and the firestorm prince.

Kael.

The name burned through her thoughts as she turned the brass handle and pushed the door open. The ballroom beyond was alive with movement, laughter, and the clink of crystal. A sea of masked faces surrounded the center of the room, where musicians played the strings and woodwinds, the music both haunting and beautiful.

And at the edge of it all stood Kael.

His presence in the room was undeniable—taller than most, his dark eyes burning through the crowd with an intensity that made the air itself shimmer. His mask, black and gold, was more elaborate than most, covering only the upper half of his face and leaving his lips exposed. It was a mask of fire, of death, of something that was both regal and terrifying. The cloak draped over his shoulders shimmered with an almost imperceptible heat, as if it too were alive with the power of the flames he carried inside him.

And as their eyes met, Liora felt it again—the heat, the force that seemed to pull at her very soul. His gaze swept over her like a predator sizing up its prey, his mouth lifting in a smile that never reached his eyes.

She could not look away.

"Liora." His voice came low, a velvet whisper across the distance, and for a heartbeat, the chaos of the room seemed to fade. "I thought you might disappear into the shadows for the night."

"I am no ghost," she replied, her voice steady, though every fiber of her being screamed to run. "I only do what is expected of me."

Kael's lips quirked into a smile, but it was a smile full of knowing. "Of course. And what is it that you expect of yourself, my lady?"

Liora swallowed, feeling the weight of his words settle into her chest like a stone. What did she expect of herself? She had long ago buried that question beneath the dust of survival and compromise. But now, standing before him, with his gaze burning into hers, the answer seemed painfully clear.

"To stay out of trouble," she said, though the words felt hollow.

Kael took a step toward her, his presence shifting the air in ways she couldn't explain. His eyes were still locked on hers, and Liora's pulse quickened with each beat. "That may prove more difficult than you think." His tone was playful, but there was an edge to it—an undercurrent of something far darker.

He took her hand without asking, his touch sending a shock of warmth through her, and led her to the center of the ballroom, where the musicians played a slow, aching waltz. The floor beneath her feet seemed to hum with life, the polished marble reflecting the gold of the chandeliers above. She felt a thousand eyes on her as she joined him in the dance, the soft rustle of her silk gown brushing against the floor as she stepped closer.

Each movement felt calculated, as if the very air bent to Kael's will. His touch was light, but it carried the weight of authority, of power. Liora's hand rested on his shoulder, and for a brief moment, she wondered if she had ever felt anything as electric as the way his presence ignited the space between them.

"You are not what you seem," Kael said, his voice low, close enough that only she could hear. The words sent a shiver down her spine, but she refused to let him see it.

"Neither are you," she replied, her gaze steady, though her heart raced in her chest.

Kael's smirk deepened, the flicker of amusement dancing in his molten eyes. "I think you are more than you know, Liora." He paused, his fingers tightening ever so slightly on her waist, and she felt a rush of warmth, of something burning beneath her skin. "And I think you're beginning to realize just how dangerous that is."

The Dance of Lies

Her breath caught. "I don't know what you mean."

"Oh, but you do." His voice was a whisper now, a secret between them that no one else could hear. "You feel it, don't you? The power inside you, the way it wants to wake up. To be used."

Liora's stomach twisted. The fire in his voice matched the heat in her veins, but the sensation was not one of comfort—it was something far more dangerous. Something that she was unwilling to acknowledge.

"I am nothing more than a dancer," she said, her voice shaking despite herself. "I don't know what you're talking about."

Kael stopped. The music continued to play, but the world around them seemed to freeze in that single moment. His gaze was intense, unrelenting, and for a heartbeat, she was caught in it like a moth to a flame.

"You are more than that," he said quietly, his voice almost tender, though it held the promise of something darker. "You can either accept that or you can keep running. But the world doesn't give you a choice, Liora. Not when it needs what you have."

His words were a trap, a promise, and a threat all at once.

Liora wanted to pull away, to break free from the grip of his gaze, but she couldn't. Not when he was so close. Not when the flames inside her felt like they might burn through her skin at any moment.

"Let me go," she whispered, her voice barely audible.

Kael's eyes softened, but only for a moment. He leaned in, his breath brushing against her ear, and the heat of him surrounded her. "I can't, Liora. Not yet."

And in that moment, she realized he had already claimed her—heart and soul—even if she was too afraid to admit it.

As they continued to dance, the room swirling around them in a haze of movement and sound, Liora could no longer deny what was becoming painfully clear. She was trapped. In a dance she couldn't escape, with a prince whose fire threatened to consume everything she was.

And the worst part? She was starting to want it.

Six

The Flames of Betrayal

The silence between them stretched, thick and oppressive, like the calm before a storm. Liora sat by the fire, the low crackle of the flames her only companion as the night around them seemed to deepen. The air was cool, but the lingering heat of Kael's presence in the clearing made her skin flush with a warmth that had nothing to do with the fire. Her heart still raced from their earlier conversation, the words he had said lingering like an unspoken promise between them.

Kael was nowhere to be seen.

She glanced around, her eyes scanning the shadows that seemed to stretch infinitely into the night. The camp had been quiet, too quiet, since their arrival. The horses were tethered at the edge of the clearing, their breath coming in soft, rhythmic snorts, and the fire crackled softly, sending tendrils of smoke into the sky. But beyond that, there was nothing but the oppressive stillness of the forest. It was as though the very world held its breath.

A sudden rustle in the bushes snapped Liora to attention, her senses immediately sharpening. She didn't know what to expect—whether it was Kael returning or something far worse—but the air around her had shifted. Something was wrong. She could feel it in her bones, an unease that crept along her skin like the shadow of a storm on the horizon.

The sound of footsteps broke through the silence, and Liora turned toward the source, her pulse quickening.

Kael emerged from the trees, his silhouette framed by the pale light of the moon. He looked as imposing as ever, his cloak rippling like a living thing in the wind. The firelight caught the sharp angles of his face, throwing his features into stark relief. But there was something different about him now. Something colder. The warmth she had felt earlier, the magnetic force between them, was gone, replaced by a simmering tension that crackled in the air around them.

"Where were you?" Liora asked before she could stop herself. The words tasted bitter on her tongue, laced with something she couldn't quite name—suspicion, perhaps, or fear.

Kael paused for a moment, his gaze flicking to her with an unreadable expression. Then, without a word, he reached for the small pack at his side, extracting a bundle of dried herbs. He moved with an unsettling calm, almost as if he were oblivious

The Flames of Betrayal

to the fact that she had just spoken.

Liora's gaze narrowed. There was something off about the way he was acting, something hidden beneath the surface of his cool composure. She couldn't put her finger on it, but she could feel it, a shift in the air, a change in the very way he moved, like a storm gathering on the horizon.

"I need to speak with you," she said, her voice quieter now, but firm.

Kael's eyes met hers, and for a moment, they locked in that intense, molten gaze. A flicker of something—guilt, perhaps, or hesitation—passed across his features, but it was gone so quickly that she couldn't be sure.

"What is it?" His voice was softer than before, but there was a hardness to it now that hadn't been there before. It was as if he were holding something back, something important.

Liora swallowed, her throat dry, and her gaze flickered to the fire, the dancing flames casting strange shadows on her face. "I don't understand. You've kept me here, told me nothing about why I'm really here, why I'm involved in this…" She trailed off, her mind racing as she tried to sort through her feelings. "Why do you need me, Kael?"

There it was. The question she had been avoiding, the question that had gnawed at her ever since he had taken her from Vareth. She had kept her distance, telling herself that she would figure it out, that she could stay detached. But now, with his presence so close, with the weight of his unspoken secrets hanging between them, she couldn't ignore it any longer.

Kael studied her for a long moment, his eyes cold and unreadable. The tension between them thickened, the air around them crackling like dry wood waiting to ignite.

"I need you because of what you are," Kael said, his voice barely above a whisper. "Because of what you can do."

Liora's breath caught. "What I can do?"

He nodded slowly, his gaze unwavering. "You are more than just a dancer, Liora. I saw it the first time I watched you perform—the way the air changed around you, the way the earth responded to your every move. You have power, a gift that could change everything."

Liora shook her head, her mind reeling. "I don't... I don't have power. I don't have anything."

Kael's expression softened, but there was no warmth in it. Only something darker, more calculating. "You do. I've seen it. And you're going to help me unlock it."

The words hit her like a physical blow, and for a moment, she was too stunned to respond. She opened her mouth, but no sound came out. Kael was watching her with that same intense gaze, as if he were waiting for her to understand, waiting for her to accept the impossible reality of what he was saying.

"I can't," she finally whispered, her voice trembling with the weight of her own disbelief. "I can't do what you're asking."

Kael's lips curled into a small, humorless smile. "You don't have a choice."

The coldness in his tone sent a shiver down her spine. For the first time, Liora realized that this wasn't just about a kingdom or a throne—it was about something far more dangerous. Something far more powerful.

"I told you," Kael continued, his voice soft but filled with an undeniable force. "You are the key. To everything. And you will help me, whether you want to or not."

Liora swallowed hard, her heart pounding in her chest. She wanted to run. To escape. But she knew, deep down, that she couldn't. Not anymore. She was already in too deep.

"Kael…" Her voice cracked, and she hated the way it sounded—soft, uncertain, like she was already losing control. "What are you asking me to do?"

Kael stepped forward, closing the distance between them in a fluid, almost predatory movement. He reached out, his hand brushing against her cheek, his touch sending a jolt of heat through her. "I'm asking you to help me unlock the power that lies dormant within you. The power that could change the fate of our worlds. I'm asking you to trust me."

Liora's breath caught in her throat as she stared at him, her heart pounding so loudly that it drowned out everything else. The warmth of his touch, the heat of his presence, the promise in his words—all of it pulled her toward him, drawing her into a world that she wasn't sure she was ready to face.

But there was no turning back now.

She was already too close to the flames.

Seven

Chains of Duty

The moon hung high in the sky, a cold silver eye that pierced through the canopy of trees. Liora sat on the cold stone bench by the campfire, her hands clasped tightly together, her thoughts swirling in chaos. The crackle of the fire was the only sound breaking the silence, but it wasn't enough to drown the storm in her chest. Her breath came out in soft, visible bursts as the night air grew colder, the chill sinking into her bones.

Kael had gone off into the woods hours ago, and she hadn't seen him since. A part of her resented the distance. Another part of her wanted nothing more than to escape the smoldering weight of his presence. The firelight flickered, its dance hypnotic, but it was the shadows that unsettled her. The ones that seemed to press in from every angle, as though the forest itself was conspiring against her.

A Dance with the Firestorm Prince

Her fingers clenched into fists. What had she gotten herself into?

Ever since that first night in the palace, everything had changed. Kael had come into her life like a storm, pulling her into his world with promises of power, of a destiny she had never asked for. She had tried to tell herself that it was a mistake—something she could fight against, something that would pass. But every time she saw him, every time their eyes met, there was that spark, that inevitable pull. It was like she was drawn to him by something far stronger than reason or logic.

And now, he was out there, somewhere in the darkness, and she was left to wonder what secrets he was hiding. What had he meant by "unlocking her power"? The idea of it haunted her, but the truth was, she didn't want to know. She didn't want to be a pawn in his game, nor did she want to be a part of whatever dark forces he had stirred up.

Liora closed her eyes, trying to steady her breathing, trying to regain control of herself. She had never been good at waiting. She needed answers, but more than that, she needed clarity. What did she want? What did she need?

A sudden rustle in the bushes snapped her back to reality. Her heart skipped a beat, and she stood quickly, scanning the shadows around her. The silence that had enveloped the camp was broken, the sounds of nature drowning beneath the heavy beat of her pulse. The rustling continued, louder now, and her breath caught as she took a step back, her body tense with anticipation.

Chains of Duty

Then, Kael emerged from the darkness.

The tension in her chest eased ever so slightly, but the relief was fleeting. There was something different about him. His eyes, usually molten and intense, were cold and hard, a far cry from the warmth he had shown her earlier. His shoulders were tense, his movements swift and purposeful as he strode toward her.

"Kael?" Liora asked, her voice steady despite the way her heart was hammering in her chest. "What happened? Where have you been?"

He didn't respond right away. His eyes flickered to her briefly before he turned to the fire, his movements stiff as he knelt by it, stoking the flames without speaking. The tension between them was palpable, a heavy silence pressing in from all sides.

Liora's thoughts swirled as she watched him. Something was wrong. She could feel it in the air. The way he carried himself, the way he avoided her gaze—it was as though he were shutting her out. She wanted to ask him what was going on, but she didn't know how. She was afraid of what the answer might be.

Finally, Kael exhaled, a sharp, harsh sound that seemed to echo in the stillness. He turned to face her, his expression unreadable. "I have to leave for a while."

Liora blinked. The words didn't register at first. "What do you mean?"

"I can't stay here," Kael said, his voice tight. "I have to go back. There are things I need to do. I thought you understood this."

Liora's chest tightened. "You can't just leave. Not like this."

Kael's lips tightened into a thin line. "I don't have a choice."

She shook her head. "Of course you have a choice. You always have a choice."

"I don't," Kael said, his tone colder than the night air. "Not anymore. Not when I've already made my decision."

Liora took a step forward, her pulse quickening. "What decision?" She could feel the weight of his words settle into her bones like a stone sinking into the ocean. "Kael… tell me what's going on. Why are you doing this?"

Kael stood suddenly, his eyes flashing with a storm of emotions that seemed to shift in an instant. He reached for her, grasping her arm with surprising force. Liora gasped, her breath caught in her throat as he leaned in close, his voice a low rasp against her ear.

"I told you this would happen," he whispered. "You're not just a dancer, Liora. You never were. And the moment I saw you, I knew you were tied to this—this fate that I can't escape. You can't either."

Liora's heart raced, her body stiff with shock. "I don't want this, Kael. I don't want to be a part of whatever this is."

His grip on her arm tightened, and for a moment, she thought she might break under the pressure. "You don't have a choice," he repeated, his voice barely above a whisper. "You never did. This isn't about what you want. It's about what needs to happen."

Liora tried to pull away, but his grip was unyielding. "Let go of me."

Kael's eyes softened, just for a moment, before they hardened again. "I'm doing this for both of us," he said quietly. "The kingdom is on the brink of war. I'm not a prince anymore, Liora. I'm something far worse." He shook his head, as if the words pained him. "You don't understand what's at stake."

She tried to swallow the lump in her throat, tried to force her mind to clear. "I don't understand," she said, her voice small, shaky. "I don't understand anything anymore."

Kael took a step back, releasing her arm as if he had just realized how tightly he was holding her. He ran a hand through his dark hair, his expression torn. "I'm sorry, Liora. I never wanted to drag you into this. But it's already too late. We're too deep in."

Liora felt a cold wave of fear wash over her, and she stumbled backward, her heart thudding painfully in her chest. Her hands trembled, and she could hardly catch her breath. "What are you saying?"

Kael hesitated for a long moment, his gaze a mixture of pain and resolve. "I'm saying I can't protect you anymore. Not from what's coming."

The world around her seemed to go still, as if time itself had frozen. The fire crackled, but it was distant now, a background to the chaos spinning in her mind. She could feel her world breaking apart, piece by piece.

And in that moment, Liora realized something terrible.

She had become too entangled in Kael's world. She was no longer just a bystander. No longer just a dancer. She was a part of something much larger, much darker. And the chains that held her were not made of iron.

They were made of fire.

And no matter how much she wanted to escape, she knew—she was already bound.

Eight

The Inferno Within

The night had grown colder, the air now thick with the scent of damp earth and fading firewood. Liora wrapped her arms around her body, not from the chill in the air, but from the raw, gnawing uncertainty that gripped her heart. She had always known that there would be a reckoning. But standing on the precipice of it now, she found herself wishing she could step back, run as far as possible from everything she had become entangled in.

Kael had left earlier that evening, leaving her alone in the camp. But his absence was not the comfort she had hoped for. In truth, the silence left behind felt too empty. Too heavy. It was as if the forest itself held its breath, waiting for something to happen.

She glanced at the fire, the flames dancing high, casting long shadows that swirled and twisted in unnatural patterns. The world felt distorted, out of place. The weight of Kael's words, the cold finality in his eyes when he had told her he could no longer protect her—it all lingered, like a shadow over her soul.

And the worst part was that she couldn't deny the truth in what he had said. There was no escaping it. No running. She was already too deep in this world of power and betrayal. She had already begun to see too much.

Suddenly, the stillness of the night was broken by the unmistakable sound of footsteps. Her heart skipped a beat as she instinctively stood up, her body tensing with a mix of fear and anticipation. She knew who it was before she even turned.

Kael appeared in the clearing, his silhouette sharp against the backdrop of the moonlit forest. His figure was outlined in silver, but it was his presence that struck her—the way the air seemed to shimmer around him, a barely perceptible heat radiating from his body, as if the fire within him had never truly dimmed.

Liora swallowed, her throat dry. The intensity in his gaze was palpable, and the distance between them seemed to stretch and shrink with every step he took toward her. It was as if the ground beneath their feet shifted with every moment they spent in each other's company, drawing them closer and pushing them away all at once.

"You left," she said, her voice hoarse. "Why?"

Kael didn't immediately answer. Instead, he stepped closer, and the heat that surrounded him seemed to press in on her like a force, making it hard to breathe. She tried to steady herself, but there was something in his eyes that unsettled her—a rawness, a hunger, as though something inside him had been set free.

"Liora," he began, his voice low and thick, "you need to understand that everything I've done, every decision I've made, has been to protect you." His gaze flickered to the ground, as though the weight of his own words was too much to bear. "I know it doesn't seem that way, but it's the truth."

The words hit her like a slap, and she took a step back, her heart pounding in her chest. Protect her? How could he protect her when every action he took seemed to draw her deeper into his world of fire and lies?

"Protect me?" Liora's voice cracked, the bitterness lacing her words almost unfamiliar. "You've lied to me, Kael. Every step of the way, you've kept the truth from me. How is that protection?"

Kael's jaw tightened, his eyes flashing with something dangerous. "You don't understand," he murmured. "I can't explain everything to you—not yet. But know this: there are forces at work here that neither you nor I can control. I've already made choices—choices I can't undo. But I'm trying to protect you from the consequences."

Liora's heart raced, her mind a whirlwind of conflicting emotions. She wanted to scream, to demand answers, but something in Kael's gaze stopped her. There was a vulnerability there, something she had never seen before, hidden beneath the mask of the prince he had so carefully constructed.

"I don't want your protection," she said, her voice trembling with frustration. "I never did."

Kael stepped closer, his presence overpowering, and before she could take another step back, his hand was on her arm, firm and insistent, pulling her toward him. The heat from his touch shot through her like wildfire, and for a brief moment, her mind went blank.

"I know you don't want it," he said quietly, his voice rough. "But whether you like it or not, Liora, you're a part of this now. There's no going back. The power inside you… it's awakening. It's a force that can't be contained."

His words hit her like a cold wind, and the fear that had been simmering inside her all this time finally broke free. "What power?" she whispered. "What are you talking about?"

Kael's grip tightened for a moment before he released her, as if he, too, were struggling to control whatever storm raged inside him. "The power that lies dormant in your blood," he said, his voice almost pleading. "The power of the earth. It's a legacy. One that you and I share."

Liora shook her head, disbelief rising in her chest. "You're not making sense, Kael. I don't have any power."

"You do," he insisted, his voice growing more urgent. "I've seen it in you, Liora. I saw it the first time you danced. The way the air bent around you. The way the earth responded to you. It's more than just grace. It's something ancient. And it's awakening.

Right now."

Liora took a step back, her hands trembling as she tried to push the overwhelming flood of emotions away. "No," she whispered. "I'm not like you. I'm not some weapon to be used."

Kael's gaze softened, the intensity in his eyes giving way to something more vulnerable, more raw. "You're not a weapon, Liora. But you are the key." His voice dropped lower, his words almost lost in the crackling of the fire. "And I've made a mistake. I shouldn't have dragged you into this. But now that you're here…"

The words trailed off, but Liora understood. The air between them grew thick, heavy with unspoken truths. She could feel the weight of everything between them—the lies, the secrets, the things that had already been set in motion.

Kael closed the distance between them, his eyes never leaving hers. "I can't change what's happened, Liora. I can't undo the choices I've made. But I can fight for you. I can fight for us."

Her heart twisted painfully in her chest. She wanted to push him away, to escape the suffocating heat that was beginning to smolder inside her. But the pull of him, the undeniable force between them, was like a magnet—something she couldn't resist. And for the first time, Liora understood the true cost of her decision.

She was already too deep. Too connected to him.

Kael reached out, his fingers brushing her cheek with an almost reverent touch. "You can't hide from this, Liora," he whispered. "Not anymore."

The touch of his hand sent a surge of heat through her, a fire that spread through her veins like wildfire. She wanted to pull away. She wanted to run. But she knew, deep down, that there was nowhere to run. There was no escaping the inferno that had already begun.

"I'm not going to run from you," she whispered, her voice breaking with the weight of the admission. "But I need to understand, Kael. I need to know what's happening. What you want from me."

Kael's gaze softened, and for a moment, the hardness in his eyes seemed to fade. "What I want," he murmured, his voice almost tender, "is to protect you. To help you understand your place in all of this."

Liora swallowed, her heart beating wildly in her chest. "And what happens when I can't accept it? What happens if I can't accept you?"

Kael's lips parted, but no words came. And in that silence, something broke between them—something irrevocable, something that neither of them could undo. The night stretched out, the weight of everything between them suffocating in the still air.

She had walked into his world. And now, there was no turning back.

Nine

The Forbidden Bond

Liora's breath caught in her throat as she stepped into the grand hall, the weight of the stone walls pressing down on her, suffocating her with their cold, oppressive silence. The towering arches above seemed to close in on her, and for a moment, she could hear nothing but the rapid beat of her heart echoing in her ears. She had only just crossed into the heart of Kael's world, but already, it felt as though she were standing on the edge of something vast and dangerous.

The air in the hall was thick with tension, the kind that seemed to vibrate in the very bones of the building, a quiet hum that spoke of hidden secrets and old promises. Candles flickered in their sconces, casting long, trembling shadows across the floor. The flickering flames illuminated the faces of the nobles, who stood huddled in small groups, whispering to each other in hushed tones. But as Liora entered, the conversations slowed and quieted, the gazes of the courtiers turning toward her with unspoken judgment.

Kael was already at the far end of the hall, standing like a dark figure against the backdrop of gilded tapestries, his posture rigid and unyielding. His cloak shimmered faintly in the dim light, the dark fabric swirling around his frame like the shadows themselves. His eyes, those molten pools that always seemed to burn with something deeper than mere ambition, were locked on her, as if he had been waiting for her arrival for what seemed like an eternity.

Liora's stomach twisted, and she took a hesitant step forward, her fingers lightly brushing the fabric of her gown. She had never been one to feel self-conscious, but now, with every step she took, she felt the weight of the court's gaze on her. The whispers that had once been muted now seemed to echo around her, the voices laced with curiosity, suspicion, and even envy. And all the while, Kael stood there, watching her with an intensity that made her blood run cold.

When she reached his side, he did not speak at first. His eyes were dark, unreadable, the faintest hint of a frown tugging at the corners of his mouth. There was a subtle change in the air, a shift in the tension that hung between them. For a moment, they stood there, side by side, as if they were alone in the room despite the dozens of eyes trained on them.

Kael finally turned toward her, his voice low, barely a whisper. "You're not ready for this."

The Forbidden Bond

Liora met his gaze, her chest tightening at the words. "I'm not sure I understand what this is," she said, her voice betraying the fear she had been hiding. The weight of her uncertainty pressed heavily on her shoulders. This place—the court, the people, the power that lingered in the air—felt suffocating, like a gilded cage she had been thrust into without warning. She could feel the chains, invisible but ever-present.

Kael's gaze softened for a moment, a flicker of something tender flashing in his eyes before it was replaced by something colder, more calculating. "You will, eventually. But there are things you must know first."

Her pulse quickened at the subtle change in his tone. There was a dark undercurrent to his words, something that set her on edge. She wanted to ask him what he meant, to demand the truth, but before she could speak, a low murmur rippled through the crowd.

Liora stiffened as a figure stepped forward from the shadows, her presence commanding the attention of everyone in the room. The woman was tall, her features sharp and regal, her dark hair cascading down her back in waves. Her gown was a deep crimson, and the intricate gold embroidery along the hem glittered in the firelight, drawing the eye to her every movement.

Liora felt the air shift as the woman approached. Her gaze was piercing, her eyes cold and calculating as they swept over Liora, taking in every detail, from the way her dress clung to her body to the faint tremor in her hands. There was no warmth in the woman's gaze, only a sharp, dangerous edge that sent a shiver crawling up Liora's spine.

"This is the woman you've been hiding?" The woman's voice was like silk, smooth and dangerous, but there was no mistaking the venom that laced her words. "The one you've chosen to put above the rest of us?" Her eyes flicked briefly to Liora before returning to Kael, her gaze filled with contempt.

Liora's breath caught in her throat, and she felt an irrational surge of anger rise within her. She wanted to speak, to defend herself, but she couldn't find the words. Kael, however, seemed unfazed by the woman's words. His jaw tightened slightly, but he remained silent, his posture straight and unyielding.

"This is Lady Sylva," Kael said after a long pause, his voice like ice. "My betrothed."

Liora's heart skipped a beat. The words struck her like a physical blow, and for a moment, she felt as though the floor had fallen out from beneath her. Her stomach twisted painfully, her mouth going dry as the realization hit her like a punch to the gut.

His betrothed. The woman he was promised to. The one who had been with him in this world of power and politics long before she had ever stepped foot into it.

Lady Sylva's lips curled into a smile that did not reach her eyes. "So you're the one who has been distracting my fiancé." Her voice was low, a dangerous lilt to it. "How… quaint."

Liora swallowed hard, her gaze flickering to Kael. She had known, deep down, that there had to be someone else—that a man like Kael, with his power and status, would not remain unattached. But hearing the words spoken aloud, seeing the woman standing before her with such a regal presence, left her feeling small and insignificant. A fleeting thought whispered in her mind, a question she didn't want to ask but couldn't ignore—had Kael ever truly cared for her, or had she just been a pawn in his game?

The tension between them was palpable, thick with the unspoken words that hung in the air. Kael shifted slightly, his eyes never leaving Lady Sylva. "I haven't been hiding anything from you," he said, his voice sharp. "You know the stakes of this game as well as I do."

Lady Sylva's gaze flicked toward Liora one last time before she turned to face Kael. Her smile, cold and calculating, remained firmly in place. "If you say so, my prince." Her tone dripped with sarcasm, but her eyes held something darker—something that Liora couldn't quite place.

Liora's chest tightened as she watched the exchange, her thoughts spinning wildly. She wanted to scream, to demand answers from Kael, to understand why he had kept this from her. But the words caught in her throat, suffocated by the weight of his betrayal.

The silence between them stretched, heavy and oppressive, until Lady Sylva turned on her heel and walked away, her gown sweeping behind her like a shadow. As she moved through the crowd, the nobles parted before her, their whispers dying as she passed.

Liora's gaze remained fixed on Kael, her heart racing, her mind a whirlwind of confusion and anger. She wanted to understand, to demand that he explain himself. But something in his eyes stopped her—something that held her back, made her hesitate.

Kael stepped closer to her, his presence overwhelming as he placed a hand on her arm. His touch was warm, but it felt like a lie, a cold truth hidden behind the heat of his skin.

"I never wanted this for you, Liora," he said, his voice soft, yet filled with something she couldn't decipher. "But you need to understand—this is the only way. Lady Sylva is a part of my duty. But you… you are the future."

The words hung in the air like a dark promise. Liora wanted to pull away, to escape the suffocating weight of it all. But instead, she stood there, caught in the firestorm of her emotions, knowing that there was no escaping the role she had been forced to play.

And in that moment, she realized something even more terrifying: she was no longer just a pawn in Kael's game.

She was part of the fire.

Ten

The Inferno Within

Chapter 10:
The firelight flickered, casting long shadows across the stone walls of the small chamber, and yet Liora felt no warmth from it. It was as if the flames themselves had become distant, too far removed from her reality to offer anything other than the illusion of comfort. Her heart, still pounding from the tension of the evening, seemed to reverberate in the very bones of the castle, a dull ache that wouldn't fade no matter how deep she breathed.

She sat by the window, the cool night air washing over her as she stared out into the endless dark. The moon hung high, its pale light casting an eerie glow over the courtyard below. The distant sound of hooves echoed through the still night, and for a brief moment, she could almost convince herself that everything was normal, that the world was as it should be.

But the weight of the truth—the truth of her place in this world, and the role Kael had dragged her into—was far too heavy to ignore.

The door creaked open behind her, the sound sending a chill down her spine. She didn't need to turn around to know who it was. She knew the steps, the soft whisper of his cloak against the stone floor, the heat that followed him like an invisible storm.

Kael.

She had avoided him for days now, keeping herself as far from him as possible, but she knew that this moment would come, that the silence between them would not last forever. And now, here he was, his presence filling the room with that same oppressive weight she had come to dread and yet crave in equal measure.

He closed the door quietly behind him, his silhouette framed in the doorway, half-shadowed by the soft light of the candles that flickered in the corner. For a long moment, neither of them spoke. It was as if the very air had thickened between them, the space charged with everything that had gone unsaid.

Finally, Kael broke the silence. His voice, low and steady, cut through the tension like a knife.

"You're angry with me."

Liora turned slowly, her gaze locking with his. The familiar flicker of heat in his eyes was still there, but now there was something else, something raw beneath the surface. His jaw was clenched, the muscles in his neck taut with something unreadable. For a moment, she wondered if he felt the same weight pressing down on him that she did.

"Angry?" she repeated, her voice barely above a whisper. "You think I'm angry?"

The faintest trace of a smile tugged at the corner of Kael's lips, but it didn't reach his eyes. "I don't know what else to call it."

Liora's pulse quickened as she took a step closer to him, the air between them charged with a thousand unspoken words. She wasn't sure what was more suffocating—their proximity or the confusion swirling in her chest. She wanted to hate him, to push him away for everything he had kept from her, for the lies he had spun around them both. But the more she tried to distance herself, the harder it became to ignore the pull he had on her, the heat that simmered beneath her skin whenever he was near.

"You've kept me in the dark, Kael," she said, her voice trembling with the weight of her own frustration. "You've lied to me, told me nothing of what's truly at stake here. And now... now you expect me to just accept it?"

Kael didn't step back, didn't flinch under her words. Instead, he closed the distance between them with a slow, purposeful stride, his presence overwhelming. "I never wanted to keep you in the dark," he said, his voice quieter now, but no less intense.

"But you don't understand, Liora. The truth is dangerous. It's far more dangerous than you could ever imagine."

Her breath caught in her throat as his words sank in. Dangerous. The way he said it made her blood run cold, but there was something else in his eyes, something that hinted at a deeper truth, one that made her hesitate despite herself.

"I don't understand," she whispered, her voice barely audible. "What truth? What could be so dangerous that you would keep it from me?"

Kael's eyes flickered with something—pain, perhaps, or regret—but it was gone almost as quickly as it appeared. He reached out, his fingers brushing her cheek with a gentleness that contrasted sharply with the tension in his body.

"You," he said, his voice hoarse, as if the words were more than just a statement, but a confession. "You are the danger. You don't realize what you're capable of."

Liora froze, her body stiffening at his touch. The warmth of his hand against her skin was like fire, and yet it sent a shiver down her spine. Her heart pounded in her chest, the realization of his words settling over her like a heavy cloak.

"I'm the danger?" she repeated, her voice thick with disbelief. "What do you mean?"

Kael stepped back slightly, his hand dropping to his side. He ran a hand through his hair, his expression unreadable. "You

The Inferno Within

don't understand. The power inside you—it's not just a gift. It's a weapon. And I've seen it. I've seen what it can do."

Liora's heart skipped a beat. The fire within her, the heat that had always been there, the strange power she had never been able to fully comprehend—it was a weapon?

"But I can't control it," she said, the words tumbling from her mouth before she could stop them. "I don't know how."

Kael's gaze softened, but there was still a steely edge to his words. "You will. I'll teach you. But we don't have time."

"We don't have time for what?" Liora asked, her voice cracking under the pressure. "What's happening, Kael? What's going on?"

His eyes darkened, and for a moment, she thought she saw something almost... fearful in them. He shook his head, his lips pressed together in a hard line.

"It's already begun," he said, his voice low, filled with an intensity that made the hairs on the back of her neck stand up. "The war. The one I've been trying to prevent. The one I've been trying to stop by keeping you safe. But I can't anymore. Not when they know about you."

Liora's breath caught in her throat, the weight of his words settling over her like a crushing wave. "They know about me?"

"They know what you can do," Kael said, his voice low, almost a growl. "And they want to use you."

A cold shiver ran through her. "Who are they?"

Kael didn't answer immediately. His gaze drifted to the window, as if he were looking for something in the distant night. When he spoke again, his voice was barely a whisper.

"The people who have been pulling the strings. The ones who've been behind the throne all along. They've been watching you, waiting for the right moment to strike."

Liora's chest tightened. She had thought she was just caught in a world of politics, of power and alliances, but now she realized that she was far deeper in the web than she had ever imagined.

"And you want me to help you stop them," she said, more to herself than to him.

Kael nodded. "I need you. More than you realize."

Liora's heart twisted painfully in her chest. She wanted to hate him for the way he had used her, for the lies he had told, but she couldn't bring herself to do it. She had felt it—the connection between them, the undeniable pull that had kept her close despite everything. And now, as the weight of the truth settled over her, she realized just how far she had fallen.

Kael reached out for her, his hand trembling slightly. "I know this is a lot to ask. But you have to trust me, Liora. We don't have much time. The fire inside you—it's the key to everything."

The Inferno Within

Liora's eyes met his, and for a moment, everything else faded away. The world around them seemed to disappear, leaving just the two of them in the dim, flickering light. And for the first time, she felt the weight of the choices that lay before her. There was no turning back now.

The inferno within her had been waiting. And now, it was time to unleash it.

Eleven

Chapter 11

Chapter 11: The Final Reckoning

The wind had shifted, turning colder as it howled through the narrow streets of the castle's inner courtyard. The moon hung high above, its pale light casting long shadows across the stone walls, the flickering torches doing little to stave off the biting chill in the air. Liora stood at the edge of the courtyard, her hands clasped tightly around her cloak as the gusts swept through, tugging at her hair and whispering secrets she could not understand.

It was as if the world was holding its breath, waiting for something to break.

Kael had not spoken to her since the night before, when the weight of their conversation had left them both broken, bruised in a way that neither of them knew how to recover from.

Chapter 11

Her heart felt like it was caught in a vise, squeezed tight with uncertainty and fear. She had known the stakes—had seen the danger that lay ahead—but the reality of it was far worse than she could have imagined.

She had known, deep down, that Kael was not just a prince of fire. He was also a man of great ambition, a man willing to sacrifice everything—including her—to achieve his goal. Yet, the longer she stayed in his world, the more it became apparent that there was more to him than the fire he wielded. There were things buried deep beneath his hardened exterior—things that made her want to trust him, to believe that his love for her was real.

But now, as she stood alone in the courtyard, she knew that it was no longer enough to trust him with only her heart. The choices before them were no longer just about love. They were about survival.

The sound of footsteps broke through the stillness. Liora's breath caught in her throat, and she turned, her eyes immediately locking with Kael's as he stepped into the courtyard. The firelight from the torches seemed to cling to him, casting his face in a warm, golden glow. His cloak, dark as night, fluttered behind him, a reflection of the storm that raged inside him.

Kael's gaze held hers for a long moment before he spoke, his voice low, rough with something she couldn't place. "We don't have much time."

Liora's pulse quickened at the urgency in his tone. She had

expected him to come, expected him to say something, but she had not been prepared for the rawness in his eyes, the way they seemed to burn with something far more dangerous than she could understand.

"What do you mean?" she asked, her voice trembling slightly, betraying the anxiety that tightened her chest.

Kael's expression darkened, his gaze flicking toward the gates that loomed in the distance. "They know about you. They know what you can do."

The words were like a sharp crack in the night air, a warning that sent a chill crawling through her veins. Her heart skipped a beat. They—who was he talking about? The ones who had been watching her from the shadows, waiting for the right moment to strike?

"Who?" she asked, the question hanging in the air, thick with desperation.

"The ones who want to use you. The ones who will stop at nothing to control your power." Kael's eyes were wild now, the intensity in his gaze stripping away any pretense of calm. "I've made a mistake. I thought I could protect you, keep you safe, but it's too late for that."

Liora stepped back, her heart pounding so hard she could hear it ringing in her ears. "Too late for what?" The question escaped her lips before she could stop it, the fear finally breaking through the wall she had been desperately trying to hold up.

Chapter 11

"Kael, what are you saying?"

He moved closer, but she didn't retreat this time. His presence was overwhelming, filling the courtyard with an electric tension that made it difficult to breathe. His hand reached out, brushing the side of her face gently, as though he were trying to reach something inside her that was buried too deep for her to grasp.

"I'm sorry," he whispered, the words barely audible over the wind. "I should have told you the truth sooner. But I couldn't. I was trying to keep you safe."

Liora's chest tightened as she tried to find the words. She felt like she was suffocating, trapped in a world of half-truths and secrets that had been woven too tightly for her to escape. She wanted to scream, to demand answers, to know everything—everything about him, about what had brought them to this moment. But she couldn't, not when every time she looked at him, her heart wavered between anger and the deep, aching pull of something she had tried so hard to bury.

"Tell me everything, Kael," she said, her voice steady despite the storm raging inside her. "Tell me what's going on. Tell me why we're here."

He exhaled sharply, his hand falling away from her face as he stepped back, his jaw clenched. "They've been hunting us. Ever since I left the throne, ever since I stepped away from the war, they've been moving in the shadows, trying to take control. I thought I could protect you from it, but I've failed."

Liora's stomach twisted. The weight of his words settled over her like an avalanche, suffocating her with the crushing reality of what they were facing. She had always known, deep down, that she was caught in something much bigger than herself, but the full extent of it was overwhelming.

"You've failed?" she repeated, her voice rising in disbelief. "How could you have failed, Kael? You knew about this. You knew what I was. What I could do. You knew what it meant."

Kael's eyes flashed with something that could have been pain, or guilt. She couldn't tell. But there was a flicker of something more in his gaze—something raw, vulnerable, something that made her want to reach for him, to understand him in a way she had never allowed herself to.

"I didn't want you to be involved in this," he said, his voice barely above a whisper. "I wanted to keep you safe. But the power inside you—Liora, you are the key to everything. They want to use you, and they will stop at nothing to make sure they have you."

Her heart sank. "And what about you? What do you want?"

Kael's gaze softened, and for a brief, fleeting moment, he looked like the man she had met in the shadows—vulnerable, unsure, and yet burning with a purpose that she couldn't fully understand. He stepped toward her again, the air between them thick with tension.

"I want you," he said, his voice thick with emotion. "I want to

Chapter 11

protect you, but I don't know if I can."

Liora's chest tightened, her breath catching in her throat. She wanted to say something—anything—that could make sense of this whirlwind of emotions, this growing fire between them. But the words caught in her throat. Instead, she reached out, her hand trembling as it brushed against his.

"I don't know if I can trust you, Kael," she whispered, the words slipping out before she could stop them. "But I can't walk away from this. Not now. Not after everything."

The words hung between them, a fragile confession that neither of them could ignore. Kael's hand closed over hers, his fingers warm against her cold skin. He leaned down, his forehead resting gently against hers, his breath coming in shallow gasps.

"Then we'll face it together," he murmured, his voice filled with a promise that both terrified and comforted her.

But even as he said the words, Liora knew the truth. They were already too far gone, caught in a web of fire and fate that neither of them could escape. And in that moment, she realized with terrible clarity that there was no turning back.

The storm was coming. And it was already too late to run.

Twelve

Dance

The night had descended upon the kingdom like a heavy shroud, the moon hanging low and watchful above the horizon, casting pale silver light over the vast expanse of Kael's fortress. The castle loomed in the distance, its towering walls outlined against the dark sky, the sharp edges of its spires cutting through the night like jagged teeth. Beneath the stillness of the night, there was a murmur in the air, an energy that thrummed with the weight of things long set in motion.

Liora stood at the edge of the balcony, her fingers curled around the cool stone railing. The wind tugged at her hair, swirling it around her face in wild, tangled strands, but she barely noticed it. The scent of smoke and earth clung to the night air, mingling with the faint trace of incense wafting up from the courtyard below. The world felt too quiet. Too still.

Dance

Her heart thudded in her chest, each beat a loud echo in her ears. She had known the moment would come, but now that it was here, she found herself unsure of what to do. The choices before her had never been clearer, and yet they were more daunting than anything she could have imagined. She had come so far, been dragged so deep into this world of fire and shadows, and now she was trapped within it.

The firestorm prince—Kael—stood in the shadows of the balcony, watching her, his presence almost overwhelming. She could feel the heat emanating from him, even from a distance, as though the flames within him had grown beyond his control, spilling into the world around them. His cloak billowed in the night wind, the dark fabric a shadow against the silver light, and his eyes... his eyes were burning with something too dangerous to ignore.

"Liora."

His voice cut through the silence, deep and resonant, a thread of tension woven through each syllable. Her name sounded different coming from his lips now—haunted, almost pleading, as though he too was caught in the same storm that had been growing between them. The words stirred something within her, something fragile, like the first flicker of a flame catching in the dark.

She turned toward him slowly, her heart in her throat, and met his gaze. The distance between them felt like a chasm, one that neither of them could cross, and yet it was impossible to ignore the invisible thread that had always pulled them closer.

"You're still here," Kael said, his voice softer now, almost in wonder. "After everything…"

Liora's lips parted, but the words wouldn't come. What could she say? How could she express the whirlwind of emotions that had been swirling inside her ever since their first encounter? She had tried to stay away, tried to distance herself from him, but the pull of his presence, the fire he carried within him, was impossible to escape.

"I don't know why I'm still here," she said finally, her voice quiet, the admission like a crack in the facade she had built around herself. "But I am. I've been here too long to turn back now."

Kael stepped closer, the air around him seeming to warp with the heat he carried. The flames within him seemed to rise with each movement, the fire in his eyes flickering like embers about to ignite. He reached out, his fingers brushing against her cheek in a touch that was both tender and desperate, as though he feared she would slip away from him at any moment.

"You don't have to be a part of this, Liora," he said, his voice raw with emotion. "You can walk away. I can't promise you safety, but I can promise you freedom."

Liora closed her eyes at his touch, the warmth of his skin against hers seeping deep into her soul. She wanted to believe him, wanted to trust him, but the reality of their situation was far more complicated than either of them had ever realized. The fire that burned between them was not just a flame of passion. It was a force that had the power to destroy everything they both cared about.

"I can't walk away," she whispered, her eyes fluttering open to meet his once more. "Not anymore. Not when I understand what's at stake."

Kael's expression darkened, and he pulled his hand away from her face, as though the contact had burned him. The flicker of regret in his eyes was fleeting, replaced almost immediately by the resolve that had driven him from the moment they had first met.

"We've reached the point of no return," Kael said, his voice filled with a mix of defiance and fear. "I'm asking you to trust me. The war is coming, and we need to fight back. I need you by my side."

Liora's chest tightened at his words. She could feel the weight of them settling over her like an anvil, pressing down with the inevitability of a storm breaking. Her fingers gripped the stone railing tighter as her mind raced. The life she had known, the world she had once considered safe and familiar, was slipping through her fingers like sand. Kael was right—they had crossed a line, and there was no going back now.

Her thoughts drifted to the moments they had shared, the quiet whispers in the dark, the shared glances that spoke volumes, the way his presence felt like a fire that could consume her whole. She had never been more alive than when she was near him. But she had also never been more afraid.

"Do you love me, Kael?" The question slipped from her lips before she could stop it, the words tumbling out like a confession. She hadn't meant to ask it—not now, not when everything was hanging by a thread—but it had to be said. There was no escaping the truth anymore.

Kael froze, his eyes flickering with something unreadable as he stared at her. For a long moment, neither of them spoke, the silence between them filled only by the distant howling of the wind. Finally, he spoke, his voice a low rasp.

"I do," he said simply. "But love isn't enough anymore. Love won't stop them from taking what they want. Love won't save us."

The words hit Liora like a slap, and for a moment, she couldn't breathe. She had known the stakes, had known the danger of this relationship from the start, but hearing him say it aloud—hearing him acknowledge the impossible weight of their situation—made her feel as though she were standing at the edge of a cliff, about to fall.

"I know what you're asking," she whispered, her voice trembling with the enormity of the decision she was about to make. "And I can't promise you that I'm strong enough to do this."

Kael took a step closer, his eyes locking onto hers with a fierce intensity. "You're stronger than you think. Together, we can fight this. We can fight them."

Liora's heart raced, but as she looked into his eyes—into the fire that burned there—she knew, deep down, that she had no choice. She had already made her decision the moment she had stepped into his world. The fire had already taken root inside her, and there was no escaping it.

She reached for him, her fingers trembling as they brushed against his chest. The heat from his body seared through her, and for a moment, the world outside the castle seemed to fade into nothing. The firestorm prince had become her everything—the danger, the passion, the sacrifice. And she was willing to face it all.

"I'll fight with you," she said, her voice steady now, her resolve hardening like the flames that burned within them both. "But we fight together."

Kael's lips curved into a smile, a mixture of relief and something darker in his eyes. He cupped her face in his hands, his thumb brushing across her cheek with a tenderness that contrasted with the fire that still smoldered between them.

"Then let's burn the world down," he whispered, his breath mingling with hers.

And in that moment, with the storm raging inside and outside of them, Liora knew that they had both crossed the point of no return. The firestorm was upon them, and they would either be consumed by it—or they would rise from the ashes.

www.ingramcontent.com/pod-product-compliance
Lightning Source LLC
LaVergne TN
LVHW020432080526
838202LV00055B/5145